LIGHT METRES

D0745329

LIGHT METRES

FELICIA LAMPORT

DRAWINGS BY EDWARD GOREY

A PERIGEE BOOK

Perigee Books
are published by
The Putnam Publishing Group
200 Madison Avenue
New York, New York 10016

Published by arrangement with Everest House Publishers.

Portions of this book first appeared in *The New Yorker, The
Atlantic Monthly, Harper's, The New York Times, McCall's, Look,*
and the books *Scrap Irony* and *Cultural Slag.*

Library of Congress Cataloging in Publication Data

Lamport, Felicia, date.
  Light metres.

  I. Gorey, Edward, date. II. Title.
PS3523.A449L5 1983   811'.54   82-19043
ISBN 0-399-50717-5 (pbk.)

First Perigee printing, 1983
Printed in the United States of America
1 2 3 4 5 6 7 8 9

Contents

MOTHER, MOTHER, ARE YOU ALL THERE?

The aftereffects of a mother's neglects
  May spoil her boy's orientation to sex,
But the converse is worse: if she overprotects,
  The pattern of Oedipus wrecks.

PASSIONATE FASHION NOTE

Is there any man maligner
Than the Paris dress designer
  With a fad?
His demeanor toward the bust is
Reminiscent of Procrustes
Yet his lightest word a must is:
  Ironclad.
To lay waist on what was hipbone
He'll cut ligament or chip bone.
  One might add
That he blandly sets his course so
As to rack the female torso
And make husbands plot divorce. O
  What a cad!
  Very Sade.

COOK'S DETOUR

Oh look!
The cook
Who always tests
Capricious
Dishes
On her guests.

She'll skewer
Two or
Three entrails
Adorned
With horned
Imported snails.
Her fey
Entrée
May well combine
Duck's eggs
With dregs
Of vintage wine,
A slab
Of crab
And powdered mace,

A chic
Young leek
To give it grace.
Her trick
With pick-
Led spinach leaf
Produces
Juices
Past belief.

Her tart
Will start-
Le any eye,
Her past-
Ry's laced
With Rock-and-Rye.

O guest
In quest
Of solid fare!
Beware!
Beware
This cuisinière.

EGGOMANIA

Consider the egg. It's a miracle,
  A thing so diverse for its size
That we hardly can help growing lyrical
  When given the Pullet Surprise.

The scope of this peerless comestible
  Must drive other foods to despair
Since it's not only fully digestible
  But great for shampooing the hair.

It's boilable, poachable, fryable;
  It scrambles, it makes a sauce thicken.
It's also the only reliable
  Device for producing a chicken.

FURBEARANCE

*"Beginning her fur wardrobe with a moleskin
stole designed in high fashion to make up
for the modest prestige of the fur, a woman
should work her way up to a mink coat just
as her husband works himself up to a posi-
tion to pay for it."* —FROM AN INTERVIEW WITH
A PROMINENT NEW YORK FURRIER.

From the mole stole
Cut in high style
To the svelte pelt
Takes a vile while
But beguile, smile.

Don't debunk skunk
While your bloke's broke
Add unique chic
With a joke toque
Try raccoon hewn
With a brash dash.
While your dreams stream
Let him stash cash.

When his raise pays
For genteel seal
Keep your eye high
On the real deal
(The refined mind
Will conceal zeal)
Don't digress, press
If he blink, wink
Having thunk "skunk"
Make him think "MINK."

PLAINTIVE GEOMETRY

How happy the hostess who finds she can plan
A party including a notable man,
    But let her beware of the grim mistake
    That many a lady is prone to make
By thinking: "If *one* name's an asset, well then,
Why shouldn't I try to get *two* famous men?
    Each bathed in the glow that his equal
      bestows
    Is sure to start topping the other's bons mots."

But joining two suns makes for total eclipse,
A notable failing of quotable quips
    Since each wants the limelight in *his* gin
      and tonic
    And, having to share it, turns dour and laconic.
At best, one celebrity falls asleep
While the other discusses his compost heap.
    As stated in Euclid's quaint conceit:
    Parallel lions can never meet.

THE VERY DICKENS

When Christmas lists appear
   Unmanageably huge
One tends to lend an ear
   To Ebenezer Scrooge.

ASSEMBLY LINES

Strong men weep and women tremble
When required to assemble
   Christmas toys
As bewildering directions
In a dozen steps and sections
   Wreck their poise

For your brain begins to boggle
When a "grommet" or a "toggle"
    Strikes your eye
And the impulse to start hurling
"Barrel nuts" and "bolts with knurling"
    Rises high.

Frequently you must determine
If translation from the German
    Went askew
Or if Japanese inflections
Might explain the imperfections
    In Step 2

And you struggle to intuit
How "A four-year-old can do it
    Without fail"
As your spine begins to buckle
And you penetrate your knuckle
    With a nail.

Yet your laboring continues
Though your muscles, nerves and sinews
    Start to crack
And you're certain you have got some
Quintessential piece of flotsam
    Out of whack.

But at last, as dawn is breaking,
Triumph crowns your undertaking. . . .
    You turn white
At the thought that children's gambols
May reduce the thing to shambles
    Overnight.

WRAP TRAP

The job of wrapping up a gift
    Is frequently less apt
To make the Christmas spirit lift
    Than leave the temper snapped
As presents slither, squirm and shift
    Like living things entrapped
While paper springs a jagged rift
    And pens go dry uncapped,
Tape snarls, bows flap, and labels drift
    From fingers, winter-chapped. . . .
But though disaster threatens swift,
    The project can't be scrapped
Until that perfectly wrapped gift
    Has left the wrapper rapt.

THE CAMBRIDGE LADY

The Cambridge lady's pleasure
    By tradition
Is in work; she looks at leisure
    With suspicion
Though her arteries may harden
While she keeps her mind and garden
    In condition.

She goes trotting off to lectures
    By the score,
Voicing questions and conjectures
    From the floor.
Having made a microscopic
Exploration of the topic
    Well before.

If she's rich it can't be noticed:
    She permits
No display of wealth's remotest
    Perquisites
And she dines in heirloom dresses,
Sure that nothing obsolesces
    If it fits.

At the heart of each committee
  That Does Good
For the world or for her city
  Neighborhood,
She's so keen on group improvement
That she'd join the Brownian movement
  If she could.

She would rather read Jane Austen
  Any day
Than a devastating Boston
  Exposé
But her mind is open-ended:
She thinks modern music splendid—
  In its way.

Though from Portland to Atlanta
  Now and then
Ladies quail before the Canta-
  Brigienne,
She looks beautiful and wise
To the presbyotic eyes
  Of Cambridge men.

SUMMERY JUDGMENT

Summer is icumen in
    And millions grow cuc<u>koo</u>
Nursing seeds and cursing weeds
    As hope springs up anew—
    Though undue.

"Last year's parsley came up sparsely,
    This year's will come through,
Also dazzling rows of basil,
    Beans and melons, too—
    Honeydew!"

Up at dawn to tend the lawn,
    They sweat and toil and stew,
Spines in knots from jiffypots
    Transplanted (all askew).
    Aches accrue;

Yet they all, from spring to fall,
    Though sorely tried, stay true.
Who're these fools with garden tools,
    This idiotic crew?
    Me and you.

IT TAKES A HEAP OF COMPOST
TO MAKE A HOUSE A MESS

"Come live with me and be my love,"
  Wrote Marlowe, but he meant
"*Compost* with me and rise above
  The somewhat gamy scent
Exuded while bacterial
  Activities convert
Old carrot tops and cereal
  To rich, nutritious dirt,
Thus proving that the offal piles
  We've lived so long among
Can be subdued by nature's wiles
  Until God's swill is dung!"

LAWN GONE DAZE

Even a sensible person gets rabid
When the bluegrass he's planted is choked
by the crabbèd.

GOURD, HAVE MERCY!

If there's anything more galling than the crop
    that flopped,
  It's the crop that has too fulsomely succeeded,
Which can make you start to think it would
    be wise to opt
   For a garden that's unplanted and unweeded—
    A feeling that increases at a stiffer rate
    The moment your zucchini vines proliferate.

For they fructify so freely that they summon
    shades
   Of terror from "The Sorcerer's Apprentice"
When the gourds keep coming at you in such
    cavalcades
   That you're sure you'll soon become *non
    compos mentis.*
     The teeniest zucchini can, in one day
     flat,
     Expand to the dimension of a baseball bat.

You can stew it, fry it, roast it, you can serve
    it raw,
  Or even try to stuff it into blini,
But there's little hope of finding a receptive maw:
  However thin it's sliced, it's still zucchini.
    So pull up every second vine that starts
      to sprout—
  The zucchini's going to get you if you don't
    watch out!

METEOROLOGICAL REACTION

There are those who maintain that a rain
    dance brings rain
   While others put credence in chants;
The scholarly crowd says that seeding a cloud
    Produces precipitance,
But all such devices are likely to fail.
There's only one way that is sure to prevail:

If you water lawn and garden till they can't
    take any more
In twenty-seven minutes it will pour.

SLUGFEST

"A garden is a lovesome thing"—says who?
    Perhaps the slug
    Whose slugfests plug
The soil with oily glue
    To mark the row
    He's just laid low
Where seedlings lately grew. . . .
Considering the shambles thus produced.
The poet might find "loathsome" *le mot juste.*

I once was told that slugs could be extirp'd
    By leaving beer
    In saucers near
The plants on which they slurp'd.
    I did my share.
    A slug, I swear,
Just drank it down—and burp'd!
Then, joyously engaging in assault,
Reduced my plot to stubble, capped with malt.

VEGETABLE PATTER

I am willing to chat, and politely at that,
    With a house plant alone in its pot,
But I'll certainly balk if required to talk
    With that bunch in my vegetable plot.

I conversed with them once, but I found their
    response
  Was so utterly earthy and raw
That I felt too debased by their crudeness of taste
  To do anything more than withdraw.

I am forced to assert that they dished so much dirt
  That the corn should have gone into shock,
But it just cocked its ears and gave wild husky
    cheers
  That set the vines running amok.

The melons and limas, those unabashed
    climbers,
  Kept cutting the lowlier sorrel,
The potatoes quite wisely averted their eyes
  But the peppers leapt into the quarrel.

The asparagus steamed and the carrots got
    creamed
  In the rhubarb that promptly ensued,
The tomatoes turned red and fell splat! on
    their bed—
  One was potted and two others, stewed.

All the lettuce would say was, "Hey! Lettuce
    be gay!"
    Causing merriment uncontrolled,
The beets said the spinach was making their
    skin itch,
    A squash laid an eggplant out cold.

And that's why conversation with mass
    vegetation
    Is something I've firmly suppressed,
Though talk may be valid indoors with a salad—
    Providing it's properly dressed.

YOUR GARDEN PLOT WON'T THICKEN IF YOU'RE STINGY WITH THE CHICKEN WIRE

When you're budgeting a garden, though
    your eyes begin to shine
  With the joyous hope of cutting down expense,
If you happen to be planting on a rabbit-
    transit line
  Your motto should be: "Millions for the fence!'

INTIMATION OF MIDDLE AGE

Work habits slack,
  Nights gay and vinous—
    What can you expect?
    Heaven will object,
Launching the attack:
  Pain in the sinous.

Work might and main.
  Nights dully tranquil,
    Attitudes correct—
    What do you collect?
Vericose vein,
  Swelling of the anquil.

Riot of crime.
  Or diet of virtue—
    Neither will deflect
    Nature's disrespect.
Once you pass the prime
  Minor parts desertue.

STATISTIC

Middle age is very difficult to chart
Since no one really knows when it should start
But a simple calculation gets the figure down pat:
It begins a decade later than wherever you're at.

RAISING THE BRIDGEWORK

When strangers shift quite suddenly from
    "Miss" to "Ma'am"
It's clear that too much water has flowed over
    Madame.

A WORD TO THE YOUNG

If you mock middle age and deride it
Insisting you cannot abide it,
    You may need this concise
    But effective advice:
Don't knock it until you have tried it.

SPINAL DISCORD

I sing a lay of vertebrae
  Contiguously clacking.
Though once dyspepsia had its day
And bouts of gout held men at bay
  The back is now attacking.

Physicians frisk for ruptured disk
  And spy along the spine,
Discreetly probing every risk.
The castanet of bone is brisk
  Above the patient's whine

As orthopedic fingers plumb
  What once was loose and limber
From coccyx up to cranium
Till from the lumber regions come
  The strident cries of "Timber!"

The flying disk and erring bone
  Encased in stiff regalia
Give legions, strangely rigid grown,
The corset's special wheezing tone.
  Ah! Such a bac-can-ail-ia.

BALANCE

A society that glows
   With a pure
      Youth-cult
         Obsession
May end up in the throes
   Of mature
      Adult
         Depression

BRINGING HOME THE BEACON

Middle age shines with delightful incandescence
As the only sure cure for persistent adolescence.

ACHING FOOTNOTE

What's so great about being twenty?
     Plenty.

INCITEMENT TO DIET

The loud repercussions of diet discussions
   Can set you to groaning aloud
By raising the issue of adipose tissue
   With which you feel overendowed.

You determine to lose, but which method to use?
   They're all couched in such intricate terms
That you long to get hold of those wise men of old
   Who sponsored the Diet of Worms.

THE CONCAVE MAN

Nutritionists stress that one cannot suppress
  The thought that a diet is doomed, to distress
    Until and unless its adherents confess
      There's only one thing they can eat
        with success:
      Less.

MINI-MAXIM

Effulgent indulgence
 In scotch or martini
May set off a bulgence
 That splits the bikini.

LEG WORK

The doctors all say
   When a diet's beginning
That a walk every day
   Is both healthy and thinning,

But it's hard to arrive
   At a method for balking
The impulse to drive
   When we ought to be walking:

From cradle to grave
   There's an absence of leeway
In the home of the brave
   And the land of the freeway.

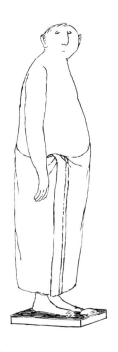

BALANCED JUDGMENT

No diet ever justifies
   The trouble it entails
Until the scales fall from your eyes
   Or your eyes fall from the scales.

PASSING THE BUXOM

When the waves of hunger lash you
  Though your loss of weight is low
Comes the urge to take the cashew
  And to let the credit go.

KNIFE-EDGE DECISION

A well-marbled steak is both blessing and curse.
With protein progressing and fat growing worse
   It's becoming increasing hard to decide
   Whether beef's Dr. Jekyll or just carboHyde.

ENRICHED DREAM

Wouldn't it be grand to join that gratified band
Of diet writers living off the fat of the land?

HMM . . .

Nothing gives rise to such wild surmise
As the peachable widow with consolate eyes.

GREGIOUS ERROR

Many a new little life is begot
By the hibited man with the promptu plot.

HINT

There never is trouble in finding a spouse
For the ebriated man with the lapidated house.

TRUISM

A woman's constant souciance
Becomes a dreadful nuisiance.

QUILIBRIUM

The iquitous girl often loses her balance
When wooed by a man with unusual chalance.

SEQUITUR

The businessman whose ways are licit
Seldom shows a handsome ficit,
   Never winters in Miami—
   Ah! but friends, his name has famy!

FISCAL FANTASY

Life would be such a nice broglio
   Running so smoothly and mok,
If I had a little portfolio
   Full of negotiable stock.
And if it were tax-exempt,
   I would be gruntled and kempt.

SOIRÉE

The gentle wives fillet a soul
    Eptly, while the men doze,
Or roast a reputation whole
    On smoldering nuendos.

SENSICAL SITUATION

Men often pursue in suitable style
The imical girl with the scrutable smile.

SUMMER CUM LAUDE

Sing ho! for the aestival festival,
  The purest of tourist delights
Which always affords the vacationing hordes
  A chance to scale cultural heights.

The Carnival's passé, distinctly déclassé
  And only the brave brave a Fair:
In hickory thickery, folks once got liquory—
  Now it's Terpsichore's lair.

The ducks and the drakes peer at waterfront
    Shakespeare
  And flee from their lakes bleary-eyed
But drama alfresco, from Shaw to Ionesco
  Surrounds them. There's no place to hide.

The cultural cult's luring all the adults
  Though the tots find it rather a blight
And tend to grow bitter at all of this literate
  Stuff with the sitter at night.

The natives, alack, shun the cultural action
  Devoting themselves in their fashion
To televised views of the sports and the news
  And raking the Festival cash in.

BRIEF HISTORY OF PUBLISHING—
FROM START TO . . .

The earliest yield in the publishing field
  Came when scribes who made marks on papyrus
Grew so wildly beserk with delight in their work
  That the writing craze spread like a virus.

Cacoëthes scribendi, in fact, was so trendy
  A *modus vivendi* in Cairo
That writers abounded and praises resounded
  For every new publishing tyro.

But today there's less praise than in palmier days,
  Since the publishing firmament pales
When the firms that once shone as its stars
    become Jonahs
  EnGulfed by conglomerate whales.

And though passion still stirs a few litterateurs
  To embark on artistic travails
When they match their finances to
    Krantz's advances,
  The wind is knocked out of their sales.

They mutter: "Damnation! Such mass publication
   Has set off a cultural tocsin!"
And they gloomily trust that the boom will go bust
   When it's trampled to dust by xeroxen.

ALICE'S VARIORUM QUORUM

"You are strange, Lewis Carroll," the
   scholars have said,
   "We must funnel you through a computer
To bring out the nuggets concealed in your head.
   You are clever, but we are astuter."

So they traced each idea to its origin
   By the sweat of the scholarly brow,
Reducing the fabulous Cheshire grin
   To a faint Oedipussy miaow.

They dosed him with physics, both meta- and plain,
   And shifted his psyche through Freud,
But Alice's charming adventures remain
   Unexplained, unexcelled, unalloyed.

MATTER OF TASTE

NEWS ITEM: *A Mediterranean octopus in the West Berlin Zoo has been eating half an inch a day from the ends of his tentacles. His keepers are at a loss to understand his behavior.*

That octopus who
In the West Berlin Zoo
Has been nibbling his tentacle ends
  Was so often queried
  That finally, wearied,
He gave out this statement: "My friends,

"I wish to aver and state
That I really must deprecate
The tone of the tales that appeared in the press,
  My actions are simple and plain
  Involving no legerdemain,
Though properly speaking I'm forced to confess
  That the inches I've nibbled away
  Have made me (Haw!) *leger-de-pied*.
Still, why should there be a publicity mess
If I choose to be used in my own bouillabaisse?

"Those rumors are idle
That I'm suicidal:
I'm mad about me in my fashion
So join in my paean
Of Epicurean
Delight in consuming self passion."

ICHTHYOLOGIC

Why do fish, who get no pleasure out of mating,
Top all mammals in the rate of propagating?

AXIOM TO GRIND

Virtue grows monotonous
Without a single break.
We need a nip of rottenness
To keep the Hottentot in us
Awake.

SHELL GAIN

NEWS ITEM: *Crabs and snails have been wreaking havoc in oyster and clam beds.*

The quahog cried, "Damme!"
Because of the whammy
   Imposed on that chamois-soft clam.
With crabs feeding rife on
His succulent siphon
   He spends his whole life on the lam,
Which makes him feel hopped up
   And all out of kilter,
So mixed up and chopped up
   He's nearly gefüllte.

And what could be moister
Than tears from an oyster
  Attacked by a boisterous snail?
A dastard who's vicious
(Though truly delicious)
  And causes shell fishes to quail.
But, bivalves, hold steady!
  Though snails and crabs crave you,
We gourmets are ready
  And willing to save you:
We'll eat those unholy
  Tormenters who doom you,
Preserving you solely
  For us to consume you.

MR. MASOCH AND
COUNT DE SADE

Oh, Mr. Masoch,
Oh, Mr. Masoch!
*Is there something that disturbs you, Count
    de Sade?*
I'm surprised that every play
Whether on or off Broadway
Seems to star us—don't you find it rather odd?

Oh, Count de Sade,
Oh, Count de Sade,
On our splendid sadomasochistic squad
Playwrights toil and effervesce,
All devoted—to excess.
They're your servants, Mr. Masoch.
Your adherents, Count de Sade.

Oh, Mr. Masoch,
Oh, Mr. Masoch,
What a glorious sick transit overweens
Any playwright who's produced
Simple childish Mother-Goosed
Fun in two unnatural acts and six obscenes.

Oh, Count de Sade,
Oh, Count de Sade,
How completely demonstratum erat quod!
When alive we were debased,
Now we're both the height of taste.
Absolution, Mr. Masoch?
No, pollution, Count de Sade.

ORBIT

How profoundly analytic
  Of his kith and kind
Is the second-rate critic
  With the frustrate mind.

HELLAS BENT

The isles of Greece! The isles of Greece,
    Where Sappho and her fellow shades
Implore the gods to grant surcease
    From tourists in those mellow glades
To which such swarms have lately flocked
That all the aisles of Greece are blocked.

Arriving by the squad to see
    The great and hallowed ancient sites,
They rip right through the Odyssey
    In seven days and seven nights,
With motor-boosted vagrant breeze
To whip them through the wine-dark seas.

The hordes who come by air and ship
    To island-hop in Doric yachts
And cultivate awaremanship
    Of all the best historic spots
So crowd each Attic vale and peak
That where on earth can Greek meet Greek?

ENCOUNTER

If you've run into a man
Who felt his old Krafft ebbing
 Then you've surely metatarsal
 On a foot with webbing.

OVERDRIVERS

Since Paul Revere went whizzing on his mission
  (A matter with which Longfellow has dealt)
The Boston driver's been, by long tradition
  Intrepid as a leopard on the veldt,
    And possessor of a trenchant
    But ungovernable penchant
For distributing invective helter-skelt.

He thinks traffic lanes were put there to
      incite him
  And he hops them with a kangaroo's delight,
Cutting fellow drivers off *ad infinitum*
  Whenever there's an inch of space in sight.
    He is singularly deft
    At signaling a left
The while he is engaged in turning right.

He sees yellow lights as urgent invitations
  To zoom through intersections unafraid
And red lights as attractive decorations
  To amuse, but surely not to be obeyed. . . .
    Tourists wonder as they cower,
    At the fender-bending power
Of the Charge of Boston's Jump-the-Light
    Brigade.

TECHNICAL ADVICE TO PERSONS PLANNING TO ERECT MEMORIAL STATUES OF THEMSELVES IN NEW YORK

Though marble may tempt you
  Reject it you must
Although you have dreamt you
  Were marbled in bust:

New York's winter climates
   Make marble decay
(Like those higher primates
   Who can't get away),
And once it gets brittle
How rapidly it'll
    Depose
    Your nose!

Then subways will shake you
   And gasses will melt you
And snowballs will break you
   As little boys pelt you.
Your bust, once august or
   At least epitaphic,
   Will start to lose luster
   And blend with the traffic.
To put the case clearly
If somewhat austerely,
    Marble
    'S harble.
    Plan it
    In granite.

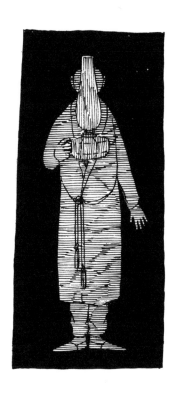

OIL THAT GLITTERS

Each sudden renewal of access to fuel
    Leaves everyone sunny and bright.
Although frequently burned, we don't seem
      to have learned
    That the plight will return overnight.
But doubtless that crisis will end when the
      price is
    Jacked to a new record height.

WILD CARDS

Everybody's living in a house of cards,
  Happily American-Expressed.
Even youth is lowering its avant-guards
  To join the shuffle with the rest.

Regiments are joining in the Master Charge
  That's blowing up the G.N.P.
Hardly anybody now remains at large
  Who lacks creditability.

With plastic credit showered on us every day,
  We feel so singularly blessed
That we never pause to wonder if we're on
    the way
  To a mammoth card-iac arrest.

SICK TRANSIT

The railroads all admit that they are down on
    The passenger; in point of fact they hate him.
A rail is what they'd ride him out of town on
    For freight is now the great desideratum.

But evidence of Pullmanary trouble
    Will never stop the proper devotee
Who crates himself and travels on the double
    In well-appointed boxcars, F.O.B.

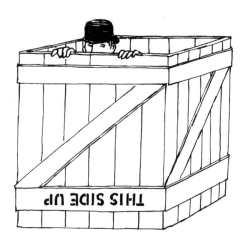

DEPTH-ANALYSIS OF MODERN MAN'S ABILITY TO ACCOMMODATE HIMSELF TO GUILT FEELINGS

The most durable wash-'n-wear shirt
Is the hair shirt.

GREATEST SHOW ON EARTH:
THE NATIONAL CONVENTION

See the scrimmage and the scrabble
Hear the raucous rabble's babble
  And the ribald rebels' ricocheting roar
When the Chairman pounds his gavel
Trying vainly to unravel
All the barking, carking cavil
  On the floor.

Strange, the leaders seem untroubled
Though the hubbub has redoubled
  And the level of the revel is a blast
For the mission, by tradition,
Of the party politician
Is to foster fuss and fission
  To the last.

When at last The Man is chosen
What togetherness then flows in—
  Every bourbon glass becomes a loving cup.
See the opposition crumble
Watch the former idols tumble
Hear that cheering laughter rumble—
  Step right up!

NONPLUSSED BY AN INCUBUS

A statesman's firm opinion must be sacrificed
   If the survey polls have turned thumbs down
For the spirit of the nation is the pollstergeist
   And the exorcists have all left town.

SPRUNG LAMB

After a sudden religious conversion
  The shrewd politician can get off the
    hook
By answering any who cast an aspersion
  "The Lord is my shepherd and I am His
    crook."

DEPRIVACY

Although we feel unknown, ignored
   As unrecorded blanks,
Take heart! Our vital selves are stored
   In giant data banks:

Our childhoods and maturities,
   Efficiently complied,
Our stocks and insecurities
   Elaborately filed,

Our tastes and our proclivities
   In gross and in particular,
Our incomes, our activities
   Both extra- and curricular.

And such will be our happy state
   Until the day we die
When we'll be snatched up by the great
   Computer in the sky.

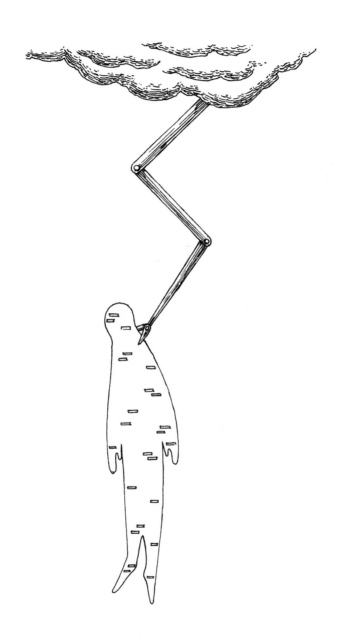

HISTORICAL SURVEY

It seems odd
  That whenever man chooses
To play God—
  God loses.

Three evocations of the Poet Laureate
of the sport, Alfred Lord Tennyson

I. THE CHARGE OF THE WHITE BRIGADE

Half the world, half the world,
    Half the world's flipping,
Crazed by the tennis bug's
    Feverish nipping.
Endlessly dreaming of
Creaming a foe six-love
Onto the *champs d'honneur*
    Millions come tripping.

Sweat-banded, ankle-strapped,
Blistered, parboiled and chapped,
Muscles tight, faces rapt,
    Eyes full of wonder,
Dancing their strange gavottes,
Hatching strategic plots,
Planning to make their shots
    Volley and thunder.

Honor the White Brigade,
Stalwart and unafraid,
Slurping their gatorade
   After a rally.
Upward and on they barge.
Sporting goods shops enlarge
Finding the massive charge
   Right up their alley.

II. GALA DAY

My strength is as the strength of ten
    My serve is in the groove,
I will not lose to you again
    As I shall shortly prove.
You've been triumphant in the past,
    The undisputed champ.
Today this worm will turn at last:
    I'm fresh from tennis camp.

III. SHOTS IN THE DARK

Sunset and the eventide
    And one more set to play:
They cannot stop until the shadows hide
    The chalk that limns the clay.

They'll stand upon the baseline face to face
    In fast-congealing sweat
Each dreaming he will serve that set-point ace
    And leap across the net.

What matter if the sable darkness fall,
    Wives fret and dinners char?
When done at last, they'll have themselves a ball
    With last shots at the bar.

CLOBBER THE LOBBER

slobs
tennis who
with have
play the
to urge
need to
the lengthen
from points
us with
spare lofty
0 lobs!

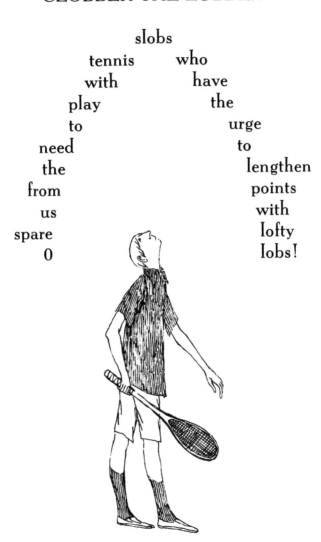

PREPAREDNESS

When you've had yourself accoutered
  In the finest tennis clothes
And been sedulously tutored
  By the best of tennis pros
And have spent long hours choosing
  Among racquets by the score
And have sat up nights perusing
  All the books of tennis lore
And have studied drop-shot placement
  With devotion that appalls
And worked weekends in your basement
  With a Thing that belches balls
And developed comprehension
  Of the principles of Zen
To make sure that tennis tension
  Won't disrupt your game again
And grown thoroughly familiar
  With the art of gamesmanship—
You'll be feeling that much sillier
  When you lose the set six-zip.

AMERICAN TWIST

A lady named May, although skillful in play,
   Had a strange psychological kink:
She never could win when she served to "Ad in"—
   Her serve simply went on the blink—
But the masterful clout that she had at "Ad out"
   Pulled her rapidly back from the brink.

It so often was true that the game-winning coup
   Was the one that she couldn't produce
That this quirk in her play gave the lady
     named May
    The soubriquet: "Irma La Deuce."

PHYSIOLOGICAL NOTE

Let us tell the addled addict as he vainly strives
    To play despite his tennis-elbow twinges
That if God had meant us humans to make
    backhand drives
    He'd have fitted elbows out with nylon hinges.

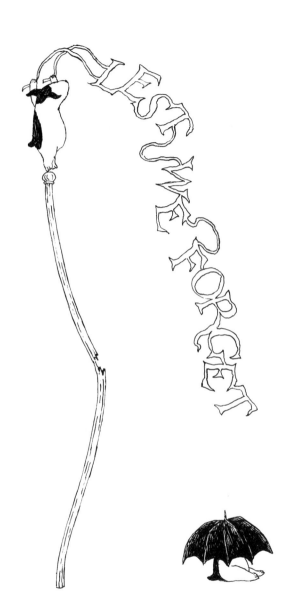

THE LOVE SONG OF
R. MILHOUS NIXON, 1973

Let us go then, in my plane
For a weekend of repose in Key Biscayne;
When the view beneath our eyes appears
  unstable,
Let us banish all incipient defeats
In one of my retreats.
Come, Bebe! Join in *dolce far niente*
If not in Florida, in San Clemente.
Let us show our heels to media that prate
Endlessly of Watergate,
That plague us with their rude, insistent
  questions.
Oh, do not ask, "Who planned or
Covered up?" Trust in my candor.

In the polls, my image ebbs, sinks low,
Buffeted by imbroglio.

But indeed there will be time
If I tough it out and never lose my cool,
Chanting my old "security" refrain;
There will be time to skim the slime,
Time to purge the scum-filled journalistic pool,
To send my critics swirling down the drain,
Time to nurture apathy
And time yet for a hundred new evasions
And time for many more "alert" occasions:
There'll be no need for me to cop a plea.

In the polls, my image ebbs, sinks low,
Buffeted by imbroglio.

But I have conned them all already, conned
    them all,
Grown skilled in arts of masterly escape;
I have measured out my life in reels of tape.
Equipped with secrets gleaned from bugged call,
There is no foe I cannot undermine
    So why should I resign?

No! I am not an Agnew, though my
    Checkered past
Includes the sour years I suffered through
My unrewarded hopes as Number Two;
Whatever small tax benefits I took
Are inadequate as recompense:
Politics require perspicuity,
Yet any man who has a grain of sense
Lays by a small and safe agnewity.
But I am not a crook.

I keep cool. . . . I keep cool. . . .
I shall have another thousand days to rule.
Shall I let my tapes unroll? Shall I dare
    them to impeach?
I shall triumph thanks to Rose Mary's
    extraordinary reach.
I have heard my staffers peaching each on each.

I do not think that they will peach on me.

I shall weather every crisis that may loom.
What if the secrets writ in milk are spilt
And detente now seems Kissingerry-built?
I shall still command the White House
Oval Room.
Disaster cannot hope to bring me down
Unless the Watergates burst open and I drown.